The Final Destination

And Other Poems

Embarking on a Journey for resillience and Self-Discovery

First Edition: August, 2024

By

Tonnie MAC

Tonnie MAC
Independent Publisher
@ 2024

For more information, or to book an event, contact:

Tonnie MAC

Email: anthonymutunga6@gmail.com

Book design by Tonnie MAC

Cover design by Tonnie MAC

ISBN - Paperback: 9798227636751

ISBN - Hardcover: 9798227636751

First Edition: August 2024

Table of Contents

Special dedication to my mother, Angeline, whose unwavering love and support laid the foundation for my dreams. I also wish to dedicate the book to the memory of my cousin Margaret, who went to be with the Lord, whose spirit continues to inspire me. The poem "Oh my beautiful Ghost" is an elegy to her.

Special dedication to my daughter Angel Olivia, whose laughter is the soundtrack to my life. She is a victim of circumstances and I wish she grows to know that she is greatest love of my life.

I specially dedicate this book to the survivors of all kinds of trauma, victims of injustice, or those who are struggling with mental health issues. May these words offer solace and hope.

Finally, special recognition and dedication to all dreamers, may these poems ignite your passions.

Tonnie MAC, which is the pen name for Anthony M. Charles, is a Kenyan poet whose work explores the complexities of the human experience with raw honesty and lyrical depth. His poems, collected in "The Final Destination – and other poems," delve into themes of love, loss, resilience, and the search for meaning.

Hailing from humble beginnings, Tonnie's early life experiences shaped his perspective and ignited a passion for storytelling. He is also a writer of short stories and Fiction novels, currently working on his flagship fiction, *'The Mysteries of a celestial Kingdom'*, and a short story collection under the title *"A Veil of Blood"*. His poetry often reflects the challenges and triumphs of the human spirit, offering a voice for the marginalized and a beacon of hope for those navigating life's complexities.

A graduate in Analytical Chemistry, Tonnie's scientific background informs his keen observation and attention to detail, evident in his poetic style. His research paper, *"Determination of Preservatives in Canned Food Products,"* reflects his commitment to addressing critical issues.

Beyond poetry, Tonnie is an advocate for social justice and environmental sustainability. His work has been recognized with publications in **Kinsman Quarterly** and **Poetry Superhighway**, as well as inclusion in the anthology *"Native Voices. – A literary collection of Emerging Indigenous Writers"*

Tonnie's writing is a testament to the power of the human spirit to overcome adversity and find beauty in the world. Through his poetry, he invites readers to connect with their own experiences and to explore the depths of their souls.

The Final Destination and Other Poems is more than a collection of poems; it is an invitation to embark on a profound journey of self-discovery and empathy. Through vivid imagery and raw emotion, the poems explore the complexities of the human experience, from the exhilaration of hope to the depths of despair.

The collection serves as a powerful reminder of the interconnectedness of humanity. As the philosopher Martin Buber noted, *"I can only exist as a person in relation to other people."* The poems in this anthology highlight the importance of human connection, empathy, and compassion.

Resilience, a central theme throughout the collection, is a testament to the indomitable human spirit. Just as the metaphorical **"bird"** in *"What a Confused Feather Falling for the Floor"* adapts to its circumstances, we too can find strength and purpose in the face of adversity. As the psychologist Viktor Frankl observed in his book *"Man's Search for Meaning,"* even in the most extreme circumstances, humans possess an inner strength that allows them to find purpose and hope.

The exploration of mental health in poems like *"Beyond the Shadows"* is particularly commendable. By giving voice to often unspoken struggles, the collection contributes to a broader conversation about mental well-being and destigmatizes these issues. It is a reminder that seeking help is a sign of strength, not weakness.

The search for meaning and purpose is another central theme. The collection invites readers to contemplate their own lives and to find significance in their experiences. As the existential philosopher Albert Camus wrote, *"The only serious philosophical question is suicide. Judging whether life is or is not worth living amounts to answering the fundamental question of philosophy."*

Ultimately, **"Final Destination"** is a call to action. It encourages readers to embrace the complexities of life, to cultivate resilience, and to seek connection with others. By exploring the full spectrum of human experience, from joy to sorrow, from triumph to despair, the collection offers a roadmap for navigating life's challenges.

As readers engage with these poems, they are invited to:

Cultivate empathy: By understanding the experiences of others, we develop a deeper appreciation for the human condition.

Embrace resilience: Building resilience is essential for navigating life's challenges. It involves developing coping mechanisms, seeking support, and maintaining a positive outlook.

Find meaning and purpose: Reflect on your own life journey and seek ways to contribute positively to the world.

Challenge societal norms: The collection's exploration of social issues encourages readers to question the status quo and advocate for change.

By exploring these themes and engaging in thoughtful reflection, readers can emerge from this collection with a renewed sense of purpose and a deeper understanding of themselves and the world around them.

"In the depths of despair, hope is the guiding star, the northern star that illuminates the traitorous paths of a tainted soul"

- *Tonnie MAC*

1. Final Destination

As this train will come to a stop unexpectedly in the happy hour,
And the station is a thousand miles more, yet not there but,
The urge to go back and book again, but how?
True, nobody can know, nobody will know
That Lions and bears cry too
And they crave just
A little love and
A hug

End!
Not yet
Not yet the end
Only the beginning to a
Long journey, that I embark on
I am sitting, looking, waiting for a train
One that will take me to the far end, dream land
One filled with ethereal culmination of beauty unseen
And in my holy mountain, none bruises another's feet on account of,
The weight that made the temple to crush cruelly in the ruins of former Egypt

None shall point a finger to the least of the unimportant, oh yes
None shall falsely accuse even the condemned of *Misri*
It is a world filled with wonder and beauty beyond
And there we will cheer for a past forgotten
Beauty that will make the soul merry
Merry for a beginning of the end
And end to the beginning of
The end of a long cry
A flawless smile
Beauty of the
End

Finding Hope in the Depths of Despair

"**Final Destination**" is a raw and poignant exploration of the human soul grappling with immense pain. The poem's imagery, structure, and themes collectively paint a vivid picture of despair, isolation, and the yearning for an escape. The train, a symbol of life's journey, abruptly halts, mirroring the unexpected and devastating turns life can take.

Yet, within this desolate landscape, there is a flicker of hope. The poet's vision of a "dreamland" speaks to the human spirit's enduring quest for peace and beauty. It's a testament to our capacity to envision a world free from suffering, a place where compassion and understanding prevail.

This poem serves as a powerful reminder that we are not alone in our struggles. Countless individuals experience similar depths of despair, feeling lost and isolated. It's in these moments of profound darkness that we must find the strength to reach out.

Just as the poet yearns for a *"final destination,"* we too often seek an end to our pain. However, healing and recovery are journeys, not destinations. It's in the process of navigating our challenges that we discover our resilience and inner strength.

Let us transform this poem from a lament into a beacon of hope. By understanding the depths of despair experienced by the poet, we can extend a hand to those walking a similar path. Let us create a community of support, where empathy and compassion are the guiding lights.

Remember, there is life beyond the darkness. Help is available. You are not alone.

If you are unable to find a loved one to share, or you might not have access to a professional, ensure to find a help line to call in your country. Support groups exist and they are ready to offer assistance.

2. When Tomorrow Comes

I'll wait for tomorrow, like the guards await dawn,
It fills with ecstasy, the desires I hanker,
The sketchy morn dawns, but with yesterday's grief…
I shun to hail the sun, as the past startles scorn,
And I curl up like a rose, on its ladder of thorns!
Wake me up when tomorrow comes.

The past ordeals sting, I've the scabs to show,
The chats assure sunshine after storm.
Yet my life dulls, it'll make thee think swan a crow!
For the world shall never soothe,
Beaten up to a pulp, you rest not till you're gone.
Wake me up when tomorrow comes.

They mollify anxiety, "With you for life"
And pledge undying love, yet leave at the sound of drums,
The battle to win, alone you must stifle strife.
For you to thrive, fiercely you show the knife,
But Lo! I can't wade the snag, with perfidy so rife,
So, wake me up when tomorrow comes.

Life's trials choke, like a snake's constriction,
Crushing my fragile fate, as the storm rages on,
Gloom lures death, like a moth to flame of light
Yet, a whisper! "The loved ones, same they face: plight!"
 And a frail call! Stop! They need you! Fight on!
Please, wake me up, when tomorrow comes.

A cry for Tomorrow

"**When Tomorrow Comes**" is a poignant lamentation, a raw and honest expression of the human spirit grappling with the depths of despair. The poem, like a wounded soul, bleeds words onto the page, each line a testament to the overwhelming weight of emotional turmoil.

The central motif of waiting for "tomorrow" is a recurring refrain, a desperate plea for a future devoid of the present's pain. Yet, the constant deferral of hope into an uncertain tomorrow reveals a cyclical pattern of disillusionment. The speaker is trapped in a prison of their own making, a labyrinth of despair where every dawn brings not relief, but a renewed sense of desolation.

The poem is a masterclass in the use of imagery. The speaker is a *"rose on its ladder of thorns,"* a fragile beauty struggling to bloom amidst adversity. The "scabs" of past ordeals and the "pulp" to which one is beaten are vivid depictions of the physical and emotional scars inflicted by life's challenges.

Beneath the surface of raw emotion lies a profound sense of isolation. The speaker feels abandoned, betrayed by promises of love and support. The world is a hostile place, a battlefield where one must fight alone. The poem captures the overwhelming loneliness that accompanies such experiences, a feeling of being adrift in a sea of indifference.

However, amidst the despair, there's a flicker of resilience. The final stanza introduces a glimmer of hope, a recognition that others share the same plight. The call to "fight on" is a whisper of defiance, a refusal to succumb to the darkness.

This poem is a mirror reflecting the struggles of countless individuals. It validates the pain, acknowledging the depth of suffering endured. Yet, it also serves as a call to action, a reminder that hope exists, even in the darkest of hours.

To those who resonate with the sentiments expressed in "When Tomorrow Comes," remember that you are not alone. The weight of the world may feel unbearable, but you are stronger than you believe. Reach out to friends, family, or mental health professionals. Share your burdens, for in sharing, we find solace and strength.

It's essential to challenge the narrative of hopelessness. Tomorrow is not merely a distant promise; it's a canvas upon which you can paint a new reality. Seek support, build resilience, and cultivate hope. Small steps can lead to significant changes.

Remember, healing is a journey, not a destination. Allow yourself the time and space to grieve, but do not let despair consume you. Embrace your strength, and find purpose in overcoming adversity.

Your story is not defined by your challenges, but by your response to them. You have the power to rewrite your narrative. Let "When Tomorrow Comes" be a catalyst for change, a reminder that even in the darkest night, dawn is inevitable.

3. Child, Weep no More

I fought a dreadful monster today,
A grisly, horrific and grotesque beast.
He mauled my heart as wolves would prey,
Claws longer than swords minced the soul.
My wife froze my soul like winter east.
"He's hungry for blood! …" Weep! Weep! Weep!

Only yesterday it ripped my hope apart!
In its grip of steel, he broke my bones,
Crushed my head like a snake to dust,
Not coz I didn't take enough calcium!
In fact, I baked in the sun all day!

Am Sure that was enough! But *basking*?
No! I was sweating.
Plotting plans to pulverize the predators!
To break teeth sharper than surgeon's blades but,
Broken bones and crushed souls!
Oh! No! No, No! … Weep! Weep! Weep!

I fought a monster but lost yester night.
Its face scary and dreary,
It ripped my soul to pieces,
With no peace of mind to piece my pieces together,
I watched with tattered parts of my soiled clothes,
The ones that clothed my soul.

It roared terror to my future.
I watched it rip my dad relics, then throw them to the gutters…
I wept an ocean!
Tears that washed my feet clean for a second.
But I could not find the soap to remove the grease,
of grief off my hands!
How would I bend to clean my feet with greasy hands!

In no time I was running scary for my life in the mud again!
Oh! No! No, No! … Weep! Weep! Weep!
Now I have no one to help! I sit by the deeper mud,
and shed some more tears,
From the empty tear glands again!

Gosh! I miss him…
I never had the chance to bide a wee!
How would he be now?
How many lives would he have saved by now?
The awaited masters in medical biology class,
But never got to graduate!

Wasn't I too young to fight the monster?
But I didn't need strength of hands to win.
I had the strong mind,
I had the unwavering spirit,
I had the good of heart,
I had the determination,
I… I… I had nothing but still went on!

 And I took a hoe! I went to the mines,
Yes… Into the deepest and darkest mines!
With a goal to dig
To dig the gold of good but not the past.
And of determination,
And of unwavering fortitude!

Today I am fighting a monster!
Today I must win!
He has ripped a heart,
Splinted a spirit and crushed a soul!
The monster has chewed my legs;
I can run no more!
In fact, I crawl on the ground,
in the mud of desperation.
Back and forth, back and forth,
The mushing mud maddens my mind!

But I have to crawl!
I have to row to the light!
Why does he drag everyone,
to his side like death?
Is there no warrior?

I must defeat!
Kill the monster!
Either way!
I have to win!
This war for us all!
Scared and scarred!
I come in courage!
Weep! Weep! Weep! Weep no more!

A cry for Resilience

"Child, Weep No More" is a raw and visceral exploration of trauma and resilience. The poem is a harrowing account of a battle against an unnamed "monster," a metaphor for overwhelming adversity.

The poem is characterized by a relentless pace, mirroring the frenetic energy of someone under siege. The short, choppy lines and repetitive refrain of "Weep! Weep! Weep!" create a sense of urgency and desperation. This linguistic intensity mirrors the emotional turmoil experienced by the speaker.

The imagery is stark and brutal, emphasizing the physical and psychological toll of the speaker's ordeal. The "grisly, horrific and grotesque beast" is a potent symbol of the overwhelming forces against which the speaker is struggling. The image of the "monster" ripping the speaker's dad's relics to shreds is particularly poignant, representing a profound loss and a violation of personal history.

Despite the overwhelming adversity, the poem is ultimately a testament to the human spirit's indomitable nature. The speaker's decision to "dig the gold of good" in the "deepest and darkest mines" is a metaphor for the process of healing and recovery. The final lines, "I must defeat! Kill the monster! Either way! I have to win! This war for us all!" are a defiant declaration of hope and determination.

"Child, Weep No More" is a powerful exploration of trauma and resilience. It is a reminder that even in the darkest of times, the human spirit can find the strength to endure and overcome.

For those who have experienced similar struggles, this poem offers solace and solidarity. It is a validation of the pain and suffering endured, but also a beacon of hope.

Remember, healing is a journey, not a destination. It is a process that requires time, patience, and self-compassion.

Seek support from friends, family, or mental health professionals. There are resources available to help you navigate the challenges of trauma.

Ultimately, resilience is not about overcoming adversity without scars, but about finding strength within the wounds. Your story is a testament to your courage and determination

4. Desolate Desires

In shadows long and solitude profound,
Stone sentinels in silence stand tall,
In the desert of the heart, no solace found… none.
Marking the stark domain of addiction's land.

Ripples in the sand, like memories fade,
Each grain, is a moment lost to the barren hell,
The sun's harsh glare, a spotlight on the charade,
Of joy once felt, now gone amiss.

Isolation's grip, as tight as our vices,
Stereotypes, like chains, that bind while twisting,
Judgment's weight, such cruel, cold device,
In this barren scape, where warmth is missed.

Yet, within the starkness, hope we keep,
As life endures beneath the arid crust,
Such is true, souls, once lost, they re-live,
Arise from ashes, shake off the dust.

A Desolate Soul

"Desolate Desires" paints a stark and haunting portrait of addiction's grip on the human spirit. The poem encapsulates the isolation, despair, and the arduous journey towards recovery.

The imagery of a barren desert is a powerful metaphor for the internal landscape of an addict. The "stone sentinels" represent the cold, unforgiving nature of addiction, while the "ripples in the sand" symbolize fleeting moments of clarity amidst the chaos.

The poem underscores the profound isolation experienced by those struggling with addiction. The "shadows long" and "solitude profound" encapsulate the feeling of being trapped in a solitary confinement of one's own making. The external world becomes a harsh, judgmental space, a place of "stereotypes" and "cruel devices."

Yet, amidst the desolation, a flicker of hope emerges. The final stanza suggests a resilience of the human spirit, a capacity to "arise from ashes" and "shake off the dust." This recognition of the potential for recovery is a crucial message for those battling addiction.

For those trapped in the desert of addiction, know that you are not alone. The path to recovery is arduous, filled with challenges and setbacks. But it is also a path towards healing, growth, and a renewed sense of purpose.

Breaking free from addiction is a courageous act. It requires immense strength, determination, and support. Surround yourself with people who understand and care. Seek professional help, join support groups, and practice self-compassion.

Remember, recovery is a journey, not a destination. Celebrate small victories, and don't be discouraged by setbacks. Every step forward is a step closer to reclaiming your life.

It's important to challenge the stigma associated with addiction. Addiction is a disease, not a moral failing. By sharing your experiences and advocating for understanding, you can help create a more supportive environment for others.

There is hope beyond the darkness. With the right support and determination, you can rebuild your life and find joy, purpose, and connection.

5. Last Supper

Why should I join your table!
Why should I intoxicate myself with,
Your costly wine you flaunt with false splendor,
But in it you slip a dose of lethal laughing toxins?
One would laugh and laud your generous tenacity!
Yet, with that fake giggle,
In the sunken gleaming eyes of a snake,
You seethe inside!

We were a number but, the undertaker claimed a few!
Am I the only black sheep that feels the froth?
Or is everyone's heart blackened with drops of seeping venom?
That corrodes the lips and you wipe the evidence?
And now you that you noticed my awareness,
You turn the table for bile to flow from my quarter
A good Samaritan, you'll offer gallons to quench the raging fire
And offer empathy to cure my irking ire!

You can burn my stiff but you won't my soul!
I will count the grains of sand in all beaches of the pacific,
But to your corrupt course,
I shall never crawl! Keep your mercy!
Every day you count a loss of a player in this team,
And blame their frivolous folly!
Holy saints you are, but the acridity of bile will burn y'all,
When reckoning of hypocritical is finally done!

Betrayal at the Table

"**Last Supper**" is a scathing indictment of betrayal, hypocrisy, and the corrosive nature of toxic relationships. By invoking the biblical allusion, the poem immediately establishes a sense of dramatic irony, foreshadowing a betrayal of trust.

The speaker is a disillusioned observer of a group dynamic marked by superficiality and deception. The "costly wine" and "false splendor" symbolize the allure of a seemingly perfect world, while the "lethal laughing toxins" represent the hidden malevolence lurking beneath the surface. The speaker is acutely aware of the "sunken gleaming eyes of a snake," revealing a deep-seated distrust and cynicism.

The poem also touches on themes of isolation and victimization. The speaker feels like a "black sheep," excluded and marginalized by a group that is more concerned with maintaining appearances than fostering genuine connections. The accusation of being the one with the "froth" is a defensive response to the projected blame, suggesting a pattern of gas-lighting and manipulation.

Despite the pain and anger, the speaker maintains a defiant spirit. The refusal to "crawl" and the determination to "count the grains of sand" in all the world's beaches symbolize a refusal to be defeated. The final stanza is a powerful declaration of defiance, accusing the group of hypocrisy and foreshadowing a reckoning.

"Last Supper" is a potent exploration of the complexities of human relationships. It exposes the dark underbelly of seemingly perfect social circles, revealing the corrosive effects of betrayal and manipulation. The poem's raw emotion and unflinching honesty make it a compelling indictment of toxic environments.

For those who have experienced similar betrayals, remember that the pain of betrayal can be deep and lasting, but it's crucial to focus on healing and rebuilding trust. Surround yourself with supportive people, and seek professional help if needed.

It's also essential to learn from these experiences. Betrayal can be a catalyst for personal growth, helping you develop stronger boundaries and a clearer sense of self-worth.

Ultimately, forgiveness is a personal journey. It doesn't mean condoning the behavior of others, but it can liberate you from the chains of anger and resentment.

6. Desert Pearl

Through the milk-white, innocent eyes
popping to stand the test of time,
surrounded by wobbly tired gait of maturity,
all sung in choir with approval of a savior born—
a stone they desired to polish to a diamond
and dazzle the dully valley of doom.

At a tender age he knew the burden he'd carry
and wasted no time to fit the shoes.
Science, art, and languages fit the tiny brain.
Bravery would mend the dire delirium at home.
Rout and rogue were never a cup to drink from.
To fail father was a fate to dread.

His radiance outshone the stars,
prompting his father to call the realtor.
Fertile soil and woolly sheep, nothing to curt the spark.
With a proud pledge he'd say, "My son, my gem,
for your shield of knowledge,
mounts I'd level for a dime."

He'd trade the harvest's bounty,
for wisdom's single seed,
forsaking a treat of meat and feta cheese.

With zeal he aced the tests with skill,
as kin flocked in plenty to merry,
while dean conferred honors so high,
he'd wield the sword of words and wisdom.
Father's golden sun. He'd light the dark slum.
He vowed and strove to shine the pearl for all.

Suited up, he hit the road to get cracking.
One said, "overqualified." Another, "a novice."
Next craved a lusty favor and a ransom out of measure.
Facing a wall of cruelty, he sailed a storm of scorn and sleaze,
and braved the bribe, the bait, the blow.
With pearl, cracked, corroded, faded, the rich fill their nests.

Oh People! You've spurned a gem and
flung it into a desert of dismay.
You've stained it with your shams and chained with cruel sway.
Once an ocean of love and care, now a desert of phantom dreams.
Moisten your pearl with trust.
Let the stream of life soothe their fray.
Wake up, People, see the pearl you recklessly lost.
Let him shine bright. Like a fane, the bleak slum will rave.

About the Poem

"**Desert Pearl**" is a stirring narrative that unfolds the life of a young man, a gem amidst the arid plains of adversity. The poem paints a portrait of innocence and potential, likened to a pearl that is both treasured and tested. It is a tale of growth and expectation, where the protagonist is seen as a beacon of hope, destined to illuminate the dim valleys of despair.

From the onset, the young man is aware of the weight of his destiny, embracing the knowledge and virtues that would carve his path. He is the pride of his father, the golden sun destined to brighten the dark slum, a promise nurtured with sacrifices and dreams.

Yet, as he ventures into the world, he is met with the harsh realities of a society that fails to recognize true merit. He faces rejection, corruption, and exploitation, his brilliance dimmed by the very hands that should have polished it. The pearl, once lustrous, becomes cracked and corroded, a casualty of the cruel whims of the privileged.

The poem is a clarion call to the people, an appeal to awaken to the gem they have forsaken. It is a plea to moisten the pearl with trust, to let the stream of life heal the wounds inflicted by neglect and sham. The poet envisions a world where the pearl shines once more, transforming the bleak slum into a place of wonder and praise.

"Desert Pearl" is not just a poem; it is a reflection of the societal rot that stifles talent and ambition. It is a call to action, urging each reader to play their part in fostering a just and inclusive society. It is a reminder that every individual has the potential to shine, if only given the chance to thrive in an environment of trust and dignity.

This poem, crafted in a language that is poetic yet clear, aims to deliver the essence of the poem to the heart of the reader. It is an invitation to introspection, a comfort to the weary, and a beacon of hope to the lost

7. Nobody Will Know

Little bear, you have surfed many storms,
Torn and shattered by strife,
Witnessed horrors, braved the cold,
But never surrendered your life.

You mastered the art of wearing a mask,
To conceal the fear and pain in your eyes,
You learned to smile and act,
To fool the world with your lies.

But, nobody will know,
Nobody will know,
The secrets that you stash in your soul,
Nobody will know.

Little bear, you have climbed many hills,
Overcame many hurdles,
Achieved many goals and dreams,
Earned many laurels and medals.

You spoke with confidence and eloquence,
To stun the crowd with your words,
You performed with excellence and brilliance,
To win the applause and the awards.

But, nobody will know,
Nobody will know,
The doubts that dwell in your mind,
Nobody will know.

Little bear, you have loved many hearts,
Given many gifts and hugs,
Shared many joys and sorrows,
Received compliments and mugs.

You showed compassion and kindness,
To touch others' lives with your deeds,
You offered support and guidance,
To meet others' needs with your seeds.

But, nobody will know,
Nobody will know,
The loneliness that you feel in your chest,
Nobody will know.

Little bear, you are a star in the sky,
A light in the dark,
A hero in the eyes of many,
A legend in the hearts of some.

But bear in mind, little bear, you are mortal too,
You are allowed to show your cracks and scars,
You are allowed to weep and seek support,
You are allowed to reveal your true colors and voice.

Because, nobody will know,
Nobody will know,
Unless you let them see the real you,
Nobody will know.

Little bear, you stand at a crossroads,
You have a choice to make,
You can continue to live in disguise,
Or show the world your true colors and size.

You can choose to be brave and honest,
To share your feelings and thoughts with others,
You can choose to be humble and grateful,
To appreciate your gifts and flaws with wonder.

Because, somebody will know,
Somebody will know,
The beauty that you have in your core,
Somebody will know.

About the Poem

In the realm of whispered secrets and silent battles, the poem "**Nobody Will Know**" unfolds as a poignant art of the little bear's journey—a journey that mirrors our own. The little bear, a symbol of resilience, has weathered storms and scaled heights, achieving greatness while cloaked in a facade that belies the turmoil within.

Most people suffer from depression, but to the world they roar in dominance and put up a face of a stone because maybe no one would understand their inner turmoil. Some, to cope with the fame of a socialite, they always put on "the all friendly face of smiles and wows", until the audience dreams of such a serene life.

The refrain "Nobody will know" echoes the bear's solitary sojourn, a mantra of concealment that shields the depths of fear, doubt, and loneliness from prying eyes. It is a veil that many don, a mask worn to navigate a world that often demands strength and perfection, leaving little room for vulnerability.

Yet, as the poem progresses, a transformation occurs. The bear, and by extension, each of us, stands at a crossroads where the choice to reveal one's true self beckons. It is a call to embrace authenticity, to share the richness of our inner world with others, and to find solace in the knowledge that we are not alone.

The poem culminates in a revelation, a shift from isolation to connection. The once-repeated "Nobody will know" becomes "Somebody will know," a promise of understanding and acceptance. It is an affirmation that there is beauty in our core, a beauty that can be recognized and cherished by those who truly see us.

"Nobody Will Know" is a testament to the courage it takes to shed the mask and stand in our truth. It is a reminder that in the act of opening up, we invite others to know the beauty of our authentic selves. It is an artistic and poetic invitation to introspection, comfort, and hope, delivered in language that is vibrant yet clear, ensuring the message reaches the heart of the reader.

8. Hate and Love in "Eden's Garden"

I marvel at the forest's diversity and sound of life,
But always drag my cold feet when,
Chen asks me to accompany him,
For the felling of trees with a knife!
It's the home of species of wonder.

Am not afraid of the beauty that bestows,
On the majestic nature,
Or dreading cries at twilight it portrays.

You see, some see the black jack as a nuisance,
And the sticky silky thistle flowers with seeds,
That seems to suck your blood dry;
Blood depleted by the biting mosquitoes,
And the vampire bats.

They cling like black blood sucking leeches,
That camouflage your skin tone,
Invisible, except for the stitching itchy uneasiness.

I don't mind the thorny plant that clings to clothes,
Or inextricable claws of the jack!
But, people seem to make a deal of it anyway,
And the story of white marula and brown berries,
That some hate while others love, only from tales and looks.

Marula intoxicates with alcohols and aldehydes.
And some call it the majestic fruit of the forest.
Sorry for the elephants who nurse bruised broken faces.

The brown wild berries attract bats and monkeys.
Some say, they dispel diseases.
Chen said that once, a bat bit a berry,
But the world paid the prize of COVID.
Was it their fault? berries are sweet! who can resist!

And when the bats got plum,
And the juicy tender muscles of the flying legs and hands!
After all, only rocks and cars were inedible.

The monkeys made away with a chuck,
And blacks pursued with passion for a treat,
And the world paid with Ebola and AIDS.
As the story goes, blacks are lazy like the jacks,
The browns, mysterious like the berries,
And the whites, they feign austerity like the *marula*!

I hate the forest - Never want to live the stories.
Gosh! the world is cracked!
Why ostracize when you can love the flourishing fauna?

A Garden of Discord: A Call for Unity

"Hate and Love in Eden's Garden" is a powerful indictment of the pervasive nature of racism and prejudice. Through vivid imagery and sharp social commentary, the poem exposes the destructive forces that divide humanity.

The poem's central metaphor of a forest is both beautiful and menacing. It represents the natural world, a place of diversity and interdependence, but also a space where darkness lurks. The juxtaposition of the forest's splendor with the human tendency to categorize and discriminate is a stark reminder of our capacity for both creation and destruction.

The poem masterfully employs symbolism to illuminate the complex nature of prejudice. The "black jack," "sticky silky thistle flowers," "white marula," and "brown berries" are not merely plants but stand-ins for different racial and cultural groups. This allegorical approach allows for a nuanced exploration of the ways in which stereotypes and misinformation can be perpetuated.

The reference to the COVID-19 and Ebola outbreaks serves as a powerful indictment of the scapegoating often directed at marginalized communities. The poem challenges us to question our own biases and to recognize the interconnectedness of humanity.

Ultimately, "Hate and Love in Eden's Garden" is a call to action. It urges us to reject the divisive narratives that have plagued society for centuries. The poem invites us to cultivate a garden of empathy, understanding, and respect, where diversity is celebrated and unity prevails.

For those who have experienced the sting of racism and discrimination, this poem offers solace and solidarity. It validates the pain and anger often felt by marginalized communities. But it also offers a message of hope, reminding us that change is possible.

Let us transform the forest of division into a garden of unity. By challenging stereotypes, fostering empathy, and advocating for equality, we can create a world where everyone feels valued and respected. It is time to replace the shadows of prejudice with the sunlight of human compassion.

Let us choose love over hate, diversity over division, and unity over isolation. Together, we can build a more just and equitable future for all.

9. Oh my Beautiful Ghost

In haste you left, not a chat or bye,
"She must be well" was easy to come by,
Yet the foe, fawn and friends mourn the guy.
Devoid of poise none foresaw time fly,
In linen the relics they dress in a tie;
Too soon you're gone my beautiful ghost.

Why do you come with eyes shining as the sun?
Your sandals levitate, the earth they spurn!
I watch the silhouette evanesce in a tinge of dun.
Was the race you promised to run won?
A home in Elysium, seems perfect, you love to run,
Yet we the jilted mourn, oh beautiful ghost!

Oh my beautiful ghost, from whence do you come?
In the glorified look of dazzle, my nerves you numb,
The feeble failing and ailing body you left in the slum,
The once faltering speech; now the melodies you hum,
Never to rise again; we succumb to the glum.
And your ecstasy glooms the grief, oh my beautiful ghost!

What lies beyond the veil of death?
What beauty hides beneath the breath?
He snatches life with ruthless stealth!
But he, the reaper, has a secret wealth,
For he turns the dust into a blooming wreath of breath.
How I long to learn from you my beautiful ghost!

About the Poem

"Oh my Beautiful Ghost" is a poignant exploration of grief and loss, offering a glimpse into the complex emotions that accompany the death of a loved one. The poem deftly navigates the spectrum of grief, from the initial shock and disbelief to a profound yearning for understanding.

The central image of the "beautiful ghost" is a striking one, suggesting a paradoxical coexistence of presence and absence. The speaker's longing for connection with the departed is palpable, as evidenced by the questions posed about the afterlife. The poem acknowledges the pain of loss while simultaneously expressing a sense of wonder and curiosity about the unknown.

The juxtaposition of life and death is a powerful thematic element. The speaker's "feeble failing and ailing body" contrasts starkly with the deceased's ethereal existence, highlighting the fragility of human life and the enduring nature of love.

This poem offers a valuable opportunity to explore the complexities of grief and loss. It is a reminder that mourning is a unique and personal journey, and there is no right or wrong way to grieve.

For those who have lost loved ones, it is essential to allow yourself to feel the full range of emotions. Grief is a natural and necessary process, and it's important to give yourself permission to experience it fully.

Seek support from friends, family, or support groups. Sharing your feelings with others can provide comfort and a sense of connection.

Remember, healing takes time. There is no timeline for grief, and it's okay to experience setbacks. Be patient with yourself and celebrate small victories along the way.

Honoring the memory of your loved one is a powerful way to cope with loss. Create rituals or memorials that celebrate their life. Sharing stories and memories with others can also be a source of comfort.

Ultimately, finding peace after loss is a personal journey. There is no one-size-fits-all approach. Experiment with different coping strategies and find what works best for you.

Your loved one may be physically absent, but their memory lives on. Cherish the moments you shared and find solace in the knowledge that their love continues to inspire and guide you.

10. Bright Light! Dim Light? Dark!

In the midst of the raging waves,
they watched her gulp the callous cunning darts.
Her crumbly heart cruelly impaled; the fate that enslaves.
So fondly she'd mask the marks.
Her soul would ache and bleed from life's glaives.
She cried an ocean for redemption from a life's perpetual stark.
In *desperation,* the *rope ends it.*

With stigma the chums looked in utter scorn,
and nattered her solitary life she so drowned in.
As a jest they'd laugh it off and know not the pain borne.
Options to content would be the faster poison to kick in.
The jeer and tough love, be strong. Would suicide suborn?
Yet blithely a random word alienates, even with the kin.
The loop finally tightens round the neck.

With croc tears the mates flock to condole.
"If this message would reach Mary in heaven;
life lost so young—" all will strive to console.
For what? She writhed in pain and longed for a haven,
but scornfully, her soul you shunned like a rotten pole.
Her tombstone, now a patch-spot for a raven.
World's cold shoulders soaked in her silent tears.

Be chaste, fair-weather friend, lest you atone.
Religion and priests you've scorned,
while the vain fanes of pretense you adorn.
In exalted hallow worship, you plead with Him
to remold the hearts of clay to vessels of honor.
Yet in your hearts of tin you curse and vilify —
you thought it was an act and left her marooned.

For remaining Mary, my soul cries to you.
Blinded by constant flopped success.
For the media, it'd hurt not to leave a cue.
Live the sacred life, gifted as a princess.
And flout their nonsensical bleats of a ewe.
I'll wait on the podium for a fess.
It's never the end—you'll ever chew the bitter pill.

About the Poem

"Bright Light! Dim Light? Dark!" is a heart-wrenching elegy that delves into the abyss of despair and the harrowing reality of a soul lost to the shadows. The poem is a stark reminder of the fragility of life and the profound impact our words and actions can have on those around us.

It is a powerful indictment of the casual cruelty and indifference that can pervade our relationships, and a call to awaken to the silent cries for help that go ignored. It is a narrative that unfolds in three acts: the birth of hope – *"Bright light!"*, the descent into gloom – *"Dim light?"*, and the extinguishing of a once-bright flame – *"Dark!"*.

The poem paints a vivid picture of a life that begins with promise—a bright light that sparks the world with potential. Yet, as society's harsh judgments and expectations take their toll, the light dims, and the individual retreats into a cloud of gloom. The once vibrant life becomes a shadow, and the darkness of despair encroaches until it consumes all. **"A rope ends it"**, was just a misunderstanding of the word **"Desperation"**, which had a cure, and a remedy while the latter didn't. Never make one seek to rearrange the letters.

In a world where jeers and judgment often drown out compassion, the poem serves as a clarion call to awaken our sensitivity and humanity. It implores us to recognize the silent battles fought by those we call friends, to see beyond the surface, and to offer a lifeline before it's too late.

Through the narrative, we are confronted with the uncomfortable truth that our actions, or lack thereof, can have devastating consequences. We are complicit when we choose to gossip rather than offer support, when we label those in pain as proud or toxic, and when we turn a blind eye to the battles our friends fight in solitude.

This is an urgent message for everyone, a call to change and to never look back. It is a plea for us to become beacons of empathy, to halt the casual cruelty that can push a soul to the brink. The poem demands that we confront the uncomfortable truth that our inaction or thoughtless words can contribute to someone's spiral into despair.

The lessons are stark and undeniable. We must strive to see beyond the facades, to understand that jealousy and judgment serve only to deepen the wounds of those already suffering. We must learn to be genuine in our compassion, to offer love and support before it's too late, and to honor the memory of those we've lost by changing how we treat the living.

11. Dead Future

She only wanted to make good the day,
And run the mile past the bay.
Their hunger riling her nerves, she had no say,
No victuals, no hope, she had to run the cay.
And feed the sprogs lest their future die!

Frenzied, she had to be, to secure her quarter.
The pain only a mother has to batter!
And get the nipper a nibble even with no butter.
The drive so formidable it placed her stiff by the gutter,
Her death would herald a future so dead for the lads.

Spirited she'd fight the course and get the bread.
Mortified and a pauper she had to halt the dread.
Learning from mater later she pulled the thread,
With courage and grit for feat she brawled the dead,
For fear they'd shun a future so dead.

Then he stands arms akimbo, his quarter invaded,
Fury filled eyes, the retribution can't be eluded!
"Why not work her field!" the vermin will be eradicated!
As the gun fires; eyes grovel but lo! killing completed…
They'll wait, wait and wait, but mother… is terminated!

Cry for Justice

"**Dead Future**" is a harrowing indictment of the systemic injustices that plague our world. The poem serves as a powerful indictment of the dehumanizing effects of poverty, the arbitrary nature of justice, and the devastating consequences of violence.

The central figure, a mother driven to desperation by hunger and the need to provide for her children, embodies the resilience and courage of countless individuals struggling against overwhelming odds. Her story is a stark reminder of the human cost of economic inequality and social injustice. The poem's vivid imagery of the mother being shot for being in the wrong place serves as a potent symbol of the violence and brutality often inflicted upon the marginalized.

The poem masterfully exposes the hypocrisy and contradictions within societal structures. The contrast between the privileged and the impoverished is stark, highlighting the arbitrary nature of justice and the disproportionate impact of violence on vulnerable populations. The question of whether this woman was killed for being a thief or for being poor is a haunting indictment of a system that fails to protect its most vulnerable citizens.

This work is more than just a poem; it is a call to action. It demands a critical examination of the structures that perpetuate poverty, inequality, and violence. It challenges us to question our own complicity in these systems and to work towards a more just and equitable world.

For those who have experienced similar hardships, "Dead Future" offers a sense of solidarity and validation. It is a reminder that you are not alone in your struggles and that your experiences are worthy of being heard. It is essential to recognize that healing from trauma takes time and that seeking support is a sign of strength, not weakness.

To create a more just and compassionate world, we must work collectively to dismantle systems of oppression. This involves challenging harmful stereotypes, advocating for policies that address root causes of inequality, and supporting organizations working towards social justice.

It is also crucial to cultivate empathy and understanding for those who have been marginalized. By humanizing the experiences of others, we can foster a sense of solidarity and work towards creating a more inclusive society.

While the poem depicts a bleak reality, it also carries within it a message of hope. The human spirit is resilient, and even in the face of adversity, people find ways to survive and thrive. By supporting one another and working towards a more just world, we can create a future where everyone has the opportunity to reach their full potential.

Ultimately, "Dead Future" is a testament to the power of art to give voice to the voiceless. It is a call to action that demands a response. Let us heed this call and work towards a world where every individual is treated with dignity and respect.

12. Beyond the Shadows

At night you call; a phantom ambles the calm.
In fright, you jump, and shun solace,
Though periodical, you scream in agony.
No one knows the inner turmoil,
Instead they gossip lesions and sores.
You refuse succor yet cry of pain unthinkable,
I know, you are strong, and the cloud shall pass.

Your pleas herald a spirit in melancholy.
The light of the day dims to a thick fog of woe!
You'll swear that the sun is swallowed by the noon,
And dread the twilight torment,
Yet it shadows your back, and rises at dawn with utopia,
You will think it's lost, but it can still be found,
Because you are strong; you'll find a way to carry on.

We should all knows it is a bumpy ride,
And the tides will toss your essence to insanity,
With a smile and a ballsy look, all scars you've concealed.
The suitor, the stranger and the foe, all you disparage with a scorn,
You are strong! But despair overtakes you in a storm,
The peace desperately sought, disappears in the cold,
And you swear that all your strength is gone.

In disdain, you'll run and run and run!
Yet not the lull you rally for a clutch to relish,
You'll search every nook and cranny for solace,
Alas! Your world curtails your peace,
But even when it is lost, it can still be found.
Face the light for the shadows to fall behind!
You are strong, and the cloud shall pass.

At last, the sun rises and breaks the dawn,
Because it was only but a fleeting cloud,
Scabs and sore will slowly turn to scars,
To remind of time in anguish,
The pits you hit scarred your face,
Yet with agility and strain, bells of victory ring,
Because you are strong, and the cloud passed.

Beyond the Shadows

"Beyond the Shadows" is a masterful exploration of the human psyche grappling with the complexities of mental health. The poem employs a traditional form, with its structured stanzas and regular rhyme scheme, to create a sense of both order and chaos, mirroring the internal struggle experienced by the speaker.

The central theme of the poem is the battle between light and darkness, hope and despair. The "phantom" that haunts the speaker symbolizes the insidious nature of anxiety and depression, a constant presence that threatens to overwhelm. Yet, the poem also asserts the power of the human spirit to overcome adversity. The image of the sun breaking through the clouds is a potent metaphor for the possibility of healing and recovery.

The use of poetic devices such as metaphor, simile, and personification enhances the emotional impact of the poem. The "thick fog of woe" and the "phantom" that "ambles the calm" are vivid and evocative images that create a palpable sense of dread and isolation. The repetition of the phrase "You are strong" serves as a mantra, a reminder of the resilience that resides within the human spirit.

"Beyond the Shadows" offers a message of hope and encouragement to those struggling with mental health challenges. The poem suggests that while the journey towards healing may be fraught with difficulties, it is ultimately a path towards greater self-understanding and resilience. By acknowledging the darkness without being consumed by it, the speaker demonstrates a profound strength and courage that can inspire others.

For those who have experienced similar struggles, the poem offers a sense of validation and companionship. It is a reminder that you are not alone in your suffering and that there is hope for a brighter future.

To navigate the challenges of mental health, it is essential to prioritize self-care. This includes engaging in activities that promote physical and emotional well-being, such as exercise, meditation, and spending time in nature. Building a strong support network is also crucial. Sharing your experiences with trusted friends, family, or a mental health professional can provide invaluable support and perspective.

Remember, healing is a journey, not a destination. It is important to be patient with yourself and to celebrate small victories along the way. By cultivating self-compassion and resilience, you can overcome the challenges of mental health and create a fulfilling life.

13. Bay of Blight and Bright

I was thrown in the night's abyss,
But the stormy clouds dispersed with bliss.
The night had fortified my distress,
But a ray from above, lit up the recess.
And I woke to celebrate, my success.
Hurrah! The dawn glowed with brightness.

Av been confused and lashed by the rain
Storm tossed and batted by the wicked reign
The crazy ride raved and ensured no gain
Yet the sun shines to ease the pain
Am refreshed and free from bane
Yes, the morning sun to the light it'll rein

A crazy ride for the swift it swept
With gnashing I did nothing but wept
Sun swallowed by the night hope I never kept
I didn't grasp, hurdles would none exempt
Soul crushed and abused I'd never accept
That the morning sun would doubt pre-empt

I finally come home free as the air
Though bruised, I stand tall as the heir
Having lost all but I kept the hair
As the reminder of victory in my lair
But as a soldier will scars boldly bare
For the morning sun shines with such a glare

I know for a fact, the dark shall return
And with veracity, losers it'll churn
Soft willed, shall mercilessly burn
As railroad ascends, to the reverse it'll turn
Better ready the horse, and victory yearn
Sometimes the dark and the light is hard to discern

Navigating Life's Storms

"Bay of Blight and Bright" is a poignant exploration of the human spirit's capacity to endure and ultimately triumph over adversity. The poem masterfully captures the cyclical nature of life's challenges, oscillating between periods of darkness and light. This rhythmic structure mirrors the ebb and flow of human experience, offering solace to those who have weathered similar storms.

The metaphor of the "bay" as a microcosm of life's journey is particularly effective. It suggests a space of both vulnerability and resilience, a place where one is exposed to the elements but also capable of finding shelter. The image of the "storm tossed" individual is a powerful representation of the challenges that can beset us, while the subsequent emergence of the sun symbolizes the enduring hope that resides within the human spirit.

Resilience, the ability to bounce back from adversity, is a central theme of the poem. It is the quality that allows us to navigate life's storms with courage and determination. Resilience is not merely about overcoming challenges; it is about growing through them, developing a deeper understanding of oneself, and emerging from the experience stronger and wiser.

Hope, the companion to resilience, is the internal compass that guides us through life's uncertainties. It is the belief in the possibility of a better future, even when the present is shrouded in darkness. Hope is not merely optimism; it is a proactive force that drives us to seek solutions, to persevere, and to find meaning in our experiences.

It is essential to recognize that resilience and hope are not innate qualities but skills that can be cultivated. Practices such as mindfulness, meditation, and gratitude journaling can help to strengthen these qualities. Building a strong support network is also crucial.

Surrounding oneself with positive and supportive individuals can provide a buffer against life's challenges.

Moreover, engaging in activities that promote physical and emotional well-being is essential for building resilience. Exercise, healthy eating, and sufficient sleep are fundamental to our overall health and ability to cope with stress.

It is important to remember that setbacks are a natural part of life. They are opportunities for growth and learning. By viewing challenges as opportunities for development, we can cultivate a mindset of resilience.

Ultimately, the journey towards resilience is a personal one. It involves self-discovery, self-compassion, and a willingness to learn from experiences. By embracing the challenges, we face life with courage and determination. We can transform adversity into strength.

14. The Burning Pan

I saw the burning pan!
Incontrovertibly sad, I tell you.
The chef was pleased with its plight.
He knew at the end he'd gain a bite,
Such low hanging fruit, he'd break no sweat.
The "prep" anticipated valuables.

The meal time came.
I grieved to see the contrast,
The incurable ailment…
That slowly detriments the economy!
The pan got nothing but negligence;
while he served his allies.

The worst came later,
Neither a reward nor attention.
The pan was thrown to dirty dishes,
And stayed there for five hours,
With its friends, they suffered poverty,
With no hospitals or roads, the children died.

Then the sly devourer returned,
With such a ballsy looking face.
Poor pan proffered silhouette solutions,
To the earlier exploitations.
He cleaned the pan with passion,
Until it agreed to cook for him again.

Now the pan inveighs with fulminating acridity,
The economy crumbles like a broken bridge,
Where no speed bumps could be erected.
The children starve with despondency!
For the extra crumbs comes from Teflon.
It hurts but who cares, when the cook's pockets overflow!

They swear someone blinded their eyes,
Yet with determination they sang the songs of victory,
When the cook juggled their future with such proficiency!
All cutlery chanted in unison for the choir;
"Who is like the cook! We want the cook!" such an oratorio!
They now find their silence for the stoical moment to pass.

About the Poem

The title **"The Burning Pan"** is both satirical and metaphoric. Cooking and politics seems to correlate. We voters are likened to a pan, that cooks for the politicians, year in year out and gets nothing in return. Promises are made and none is fulfilled. I once saw a meme, where one sanitary truck; precisely a honey sucker, was labeled "full of political promises" which would translate to mean, Political promises are "the contents of the honey sucker". They have no value, and any person should desist from banking on them

The poem is a searing indictment of political exploitation and the complacency of the electorate, masterfully encapsulated in the metaphor of kitchenware. The poem is a clarion call to the 'pans' of society—the voters—to awaken from their slumber and recognize the cyclical abuse they endure at the hands of the 'chef'—the politician. It is a poignant reminder that the instruments of change lie within the grasp of those who are all too often considered dispensable.

The poem's beauty lies in its stark imagery and the raw truth it unveils. It is a narrative that resonates with the disenfranchised and the marginalized, painting a vivid picture of neglect and betrayal. The pan, once an agent of nourishment, becomes a symbol of sacrifice, receiving nothing but scorn for its service. The chef's actions reflect a deeper malaise—a system that rewards the few at the expense of the many, leaving the vulnerable to languish in poverty and despair.

Beyond its immediate message, the poem also speaks to the broader theme of awakening and empowerment. It urges the 'pans' to rise with reason, to refuse to be expendable, and to demand the respect and consideration they deserve. It is a call to action for the silent majority to find their voice and to challenge the status quo that has long exploited their trust and labor.

In the contemporary context, "The Burning Pan" is as relevant as ever. It is a reflection of the global struggle against inequality and the fight for social justice. The poem's significance extends beyond the borders of Africa, echoing the sentiments of oppressed populations worldwide who yearn for a fairer distribution of wealth and opportunity.

The poem is a lyrical masterpiece of artistic expression, igniting the heart with the fire of love, the rhetoric of revolution, and the poetry of protest. It is a work that should not only be read but also heeded—a testament to the enduring spirit of those who refuse to be silenced or sidelined. "The Burning Pan" is a beacon of hope for a brighter future, where the pans of the world are no longer burned but cherished for the sustenance they provide.

15. Obliteration

He was too lazy to rise by the clock,
Too lazy to fix the leaking roof,
Too lazy to clean the house!
Resident chief-mouse organized a party,
Dancing, cheering, jeering, steering! Yeah!
Happy for the house they pay no rent.
And with a tin by the pointy teeth, they hop and jump!
Ting! Ting! Ting! On the floor, the empty can hit!

Laid trap snapped the toe by the bed side, ouch!
He is too lazy but afraid to share the bed with a mouse!

They were too lazy to till the lands for sustenance,
Too lazy to keep the kids in check,
But the freebase in the nostrils.
None was shaken when
Wealth beat a hasty retreat and
Thuggery took the toll,
As were per the course.

The young made homes along
The once beautiful boulevards.
Because they were too lazy, destined mothers
paraded for sampling,
As immorality militated the populace,
The rot of laziness flaunted the air.

Teachers, too lazy to teach!
Vicars, too lazy to pray!
And police too lazy to man!

Money blinded the eyes,
Money deafened the ears,
To cries of the needy.
Bushes and slums dispelled diseases,
Hospitals housed the dying.

We are too lazy to change with change
When time changes the change,
In roaring rambles of hurricanes
And howling woos of tornados,
We take the bunker.

In the slumming slashes of tsunamis
And crackling crunches of earthquake,
We count the dead.
In the swooshing swishes of avalanche
And squishing mudslides,
We hold vain conventions.

Fossil remains, ancient fauna
Drives the turbines for an electric car;
Clean energy?
As blazing fiery orb in the cloudless sky
Bakes the wetlands of savanna;
Daring death!

Too lazy to mine the field,
But nuke the borders for pride,
Now, they wallow in despair,
And swallow dismay,
As they wobble to destruction and death.

Death! Starvation! Suffocation!
Until you, and he, yes, we, stop the laze:
Salvation!

Ignorance is a matter of indifference
Apathy, and indolence:
Obliteration!

Stop the drowse and atone for sins
Against mother,
She was green but we painted brown and grey
With haze of laze,
The refreshing, the serene, the calming,
With loaf, it now chokes and corrodes.

Wasn't it better to keep the white rhino,
Than kill for sport and theory dose?
Mother bleeds red with blood of the weak,
We exploit in cupidity.

But the sun shall rise with rays to lead
The diligent,
Stop the fritter, and the dawdle,
And tame the wind, the sun and sea
For energy.
The greed, the lust and pout,
We can trade for love and poise
For Elysium
For the peace to keep, amity we farm
And laze we ease.

Awareness is a matter of interest
Empathy, and diligence: Liberation!

Society's Self-Destruction hit Button

"Obliteration" stands as a solitary beacon, illuminating the pervasive shadow of indolence that threatens to engulf our contemporary existence. This poem, resonates with a universal relevance, transcending the confines of any identify groups, comfort and ignorance. It calls to arms every available being to play their part to make the world a better place.

The poem's thematic core is an incisive critique of the lethargy that permeates every stratum of society—from the individual's personal sphere to the global stage. It paints a vivid tableau of the consequences wrought by inaction, where the unchecked proliferation of apathy leads to societal decay, environmental degradation, and the erosion of moral values.

Yet, "Obliteration" is not content to merely diagnose the ills of the world. It is a clarion call to action, a plea for the awakening of the human spirit. The poem implores its readers to cast off the chains of laziness, to embrace the mantle of change, and to actively participate in the crafting of a new epoch marked by diligence, empathy, and environmental stewardship.

The significance of this poem lies in its ability to speak to the heart of today's challenges. It holds up a mirror to the reader, demanding a reckoning with the stark reality of our times. The lessons it imparts are manifold: the necessity of personal responsibility, the power of collective action, and the imperative to safeguard our planet for future generations.

The urgency of the poem's message is accentuated by the pressing environmental crises that define our era. It is a poignant reminder that the time for debate has passed, and the moment for decisive action has arrived. "Obliteration" serves as a testament to the resilience of nature and the indomitable will of those who strive to protect it.

It is a poem that demands to be shared, to be discussed, and to be acted upon. It is a piece of literature that has the power to inspire, to motivate, and to catalyze change. In the end, "Obliteration" is more than a poem—it is a movement, a philosophy, and a beacon of hope for a world in dire need of transformation.

16. Not Just a Broken Reed

There's hope for a mushroom trampled,
If they persist to grow, their spores are gushed.
Such is the tale the sacrosanct pilgrim will say.
Yet they'll grapple with a gamble for afloat to stay
"It is finished..." like the messiah they will gripe,
And abandon the task with time unripe,
They know not a closed chapter is hard to remake.

"Never again", you have asserted with finality,
Cocooned, you've enshrouded yourself from reality,
Yet you pelt the adversary with darts of bane,
With indelible ink, you've inscribed the heart with pain,
Libertine! Given the show, you'd let everyone know,
To shun would be better, the pain will reduce, but no!
A closed chapter is hard to remake.

Like a leaking urn your heart bleeds,
You scuffle with hurt; for peace your soul pleads,
Extended hands you hotly rebuff with incertitude,
Any attempt to reanimate will be met with ingratitude,
Your soul has turned black with contempt,
Soon the spirit dies, albeit love, hate you do not preempt,
For a closed chapter is hard to remake.

Prepare the ink and indulge in change,
Embrace diversity and virtues round you shall range,
Only when you open the book, someone will read,
Accept to fall at times; you are a broken reed,
Positivity in life, is the real medicine for the soul,
Open up and devote to control,
The chapter of your life for a bid to remake!

About the Poem

"Not Just a Broken Reed" is an eloquent soliloquy that speaks to the resilience of the human spirit amidst the tempests of life. It is a moving reminder that the pages of our lives are not bound by the ink of past sorrows. The poem serves as a beacon of hope for those who have retreated into the solitude of their pain, sealing themselves away like a closed book, unread and untouched. Some are those who we look up to, to provide the sacrosanct pilgrimage, and they do it perfectly, but within their souls, is doubt they cannot pre-empt. They wear a rock of a face to be a beacon of hope yet they writhe in agony. Their books are closed and finalized. They think their story is done. Their only purpose is to take the flock to pastures they can never consume.

It is a poetic narrative that captures the essence of struggle, the sting of pain, and the cloak of despair that often shrouds the soul. Yet, within its stanzas lies a profound message of hope, a clarion call to those who have been trampled by life's merciless march.

The words are a gentle yet powerful exhortation to those who have been wounded by life's trials, urging them to unfurl the pages of their being and to allow the world to bear witness to their story. It is a call to recognize that even amidst the chaos of confused lines and chapters marred by hurt, there exists the opportunity to take up the pen once more and to author a narrative of healing and growth.

Through the metaphor of the broken reed, the poem imparts a profound truth: that our fractures do not define us, nor do they diminish our worth. Instead, they serve as junctions where new paths can be forged, where the melody of our existence can find its harmony once again. It is a declaration that hope is never lost, that redemption is always within reach, and that the act of opening up is the first step toward rewriting the chapters of our lives.

In essence, "Not Just a Broken Reed" is an ode to the resilience of the human heart, a celebration of the courage it takes to reveal one's innermost self. It is a work that resonates with the silent struggles of many, offering solace and strength to those who fear their book may never be read. Let this poem be a reminder that it is never too late to turn the page, to begin anew, and to craft a tale of triumph that echoes beyond the shadows of yesteryear. For in the end, we are all authors of our own destiny, capable of penning a story that shines with the brilliance of hope reborn.

To read "Not Just a Broken Reed" is to embark on a journey of self-discovery, to confront the darkness within, and to emerge with a renewed sense of purpose. It is a poem that transcends the boundaries of language and culture, touching the core of what it means to be human. It is a call to awaken, to rise, and to remake the chapters of our existence with the ink of hope and the quill of resilience. For in the end, we are all more than just broken reeds—we are the architects of our own destinies, capable of creating our own art of triumph from the colors of our trials.

17. Whispers

You might say, "I long to chase this path,
As far as it can go, to witness, feel and join,
The adventures of the wanderers.
I want to mimic them, and do as they do.
To dance as they dance and cry when they cry.
I want to see their sun of joy and pain,
When it rises and sets.

Their ways are trendy,
They speak and allies thunder with ovation
They appear and their peers cheer!
The world knows their names
I will endure no more solitude!
Boredom gnaws my soul; I want to go now!"

But heed me, friend,
Can you flourish in this dance of shadows!
Where humanity lies buried in the past?
Behold! blood of innocent flows like a stream,
In the hands of gannets who scour every corner
To feed their greed, they loot and kill
And drink the stranger's wine
They are vultures that feast on the dead
The path swarms with scavengers,
who brawls for your breath!

A pack of wolves will prowl in scores,
And shower you with flattery, even worship
They will sway to your tune with glee
But trap you in eternal bondage
You'll be their puppet on a string,
Some will chatter your poverty
And scorn your former clemency.

Listen, my dear friend Stop staring at me,
March on, you do not see the way, I know
But march on! march through this fog of reality
Open your ears wide, listen to the whispering voice

To the faint utterance in the still wind
Shun easy goings, my friend,
The path is riddled with traps
Dodge them and stride ahead
You might finally enjoy,
A taste of honey beyond joy,
Living is no piece of cake!

About the Poem

I wrote this poem in 2007, as a tribute to my mother, who taught me valuable lessons about life and how to avoid falling into the traps of easy goings. She always encouraged me to listen to the whispering voice of wisdom and to march on through the fog of reality. This poem is a reflection of her influence and guidance, as well as a reminder to myself and other young adults who are tempted to experiment with everything without considering the consequences.

"Whispers" is a profound and introspective poem that serves as a beacon of wisdom amidst the cacophony of life's temptations. My mother's sage advice echoes through the verses as a guiding light for me and others who are young and restless. The poem is a master of caution and courage, lacing together the allure of worldly pursuits with the stark reality of their potential pitfalls.

My essence lies in the contrast between the seductive call of the world and the gentle, yet firm, whispers of wisdom. It captures the internal struggle of a youth, torn between the desire for adventure and the need for prudence. The mother's voice emerges as a symbol of enduring guidance, her whispers a constant reminder to tread carefully on life's treacherous path.

Through vivid imagery and poignant metaphors, the poem educates and inspires, urging its readers to listen to the faint utterances of wisdom that often go unheard. It is a call to march on through the fog of reality, to dodge the traps laid by the wolves of deception, and to strive for a taste of honey beyond the transient joys of existence.

"Whispers" is not just a poem; it is a lesson in resilience and discernment. It is a reminder that living is indeed no piece of cake, but with the whispers of wisdom to guide us, we can navigate the complexities of life with a sense of purpose and hope. The poem is a testament to the power of maternal influence and the enduring impact of the lessons imparted by those who have walked the path before us. It is a work that resonates with the spirit of an entire generation, seeking to make sense of the world while holding fast to the values that will lead them to a brighter future.

18. The Fogged Mirror

I see myself in the misty mirror,
A face of peace and purity,
A perfect portrait of my soul,
A serene, sublime, saintly sight,
I can't tear my eyes from it,
But it only makes me blind.

I see another self behind me,
A corrodible horrible decay,
Of rotten reflection of my vice,
And gruesome ghastly grin,
And the feel of tug from the glass,
But it only makes me bleed.

Oh, how I dread to be like them,
To wear this dreadful skin,
Oh, how I crave to be like this,
To taste this sweet sin,
But the fogged mirror fools me,
It shows me what I'm not and what I am.

I feel a push from both sides,
A storm within my mind,
A clash between the familiar divine and,
The unfamiliar distorted,
I moan and groan in sweet agony,
But it only makes me deaf.

Who will lose this battle?
Who will forfeit my fate?
Who will break my destiny?
Who will unseal my state?
The fogged mirror fools me,
It tells me what I fear and what I want.

I don't know how to resist,
I don't know how to escape,
I don't know how to deny,
I don't know how to embrace,
The fogged mirror fools me,
It merges the lines between the evil and the good.

About the Poem

"The Fogged Mirror" is a profound exploration of the duality within the human spirit, a ` speaker — and by extension, the reader — caught in a tempest of moral ambiguity.

The speaker's yearning for both sanctity and sin is palpable, a testament to the complex nature of desire and conscience. The fogged mirror does not merely reflect; it distorts, confuses, and ultimately, fools. It blurs the lines between good and evil, casting doubt on the very essence of identity and choice.

Who will emerge victorious in this internal skirmish? The poem leaves us pondering the fate of the speaker's soul, the outcome of the battle veiled in the mist of the mirror. It is a reminder that the choices we make are often shrouded in uncertainty, and the path to self-realization is fraught with challenges.

The poem's message resonates with urgency, imploring us to confront our innermost selves, to recognize the mirrors in our lives that shape our perceptions. It calls for introspection, for the courage to face our own reflections, and to discern the truth amidst the fog.

In its rich and evocative language, "The Fogged Mirror" serves as a beacon for those seeking clarity. It is a poetic journey that compels us to examine the depths of our being, to embrace our complexities, and to strive for a balance between the light and the darkness that resides within us.

19. The Nonpareil Supple Power

You are the springs of nature,
A drop with value unmatched
The flow, the shape,
The rise, the fall, the gentle rain,
A whisper of the frost in the wind
And the soothing dew
The raging storm,
And the ocean blue

Such stillness of the lake,
The calmness of the night
An echo of the owl's howl in the cold
The run and glide of the river,
The dynamism of light
Patience of the glacier,
But fury in storm endurances time
Rush of the avalanches carving the ridge

I see the power of creation
And a force of destruction
Even constructive at times
It is a beauty of nature's design
The art of perfection
A master to the school
A school for the old and young
To catch a drink, and breathe power

H and O: yin and yang of nature
Two parents; the fuel and fan of fire
But, union unites the very rivalry
And you - the product-
Douse the fire they ignite
Quench our rage
Teach us suppleness
And harmony to bridge the ridge of adversity

About the Poem

"The Nonpareil Supple Power" is a poetic testament to the unrivaled strength and versatility of water, a force that shapes our world and mirrors the qualities we aspire to embody. This poem is a masterclass in allegory, drawing parallels between the fluidity of water and the fluidity of human potential.

The Essence of Fluidity and Purpose: - "The Nonpareil Supple Power" extols the virtues of water, an unmatched force in nature that exemplifies *suppleness and adaptability*. It is a metaphor for the *strength found in gentleness, the impact of patience,* and the *beauty of yielding*. Water's dance—a union of hydrogen and oxygen—is a testament to the alchemy of harmony that can arise from the union of rivals, much like nations finding peace in collaboration.

Water as the Embodiment of Power: - Water, in its myriad forms, is a living lesson in adaptability and impact. From the gentle caress of rain to the mighty roar of the ocean, water exemplifies the true essence of power—not in rigidity, but in its ability to conform, move, and persist.

The Duality of Water's Influence: - The poem captures the duality of water's influence—as a creator and a destroyer, a nurturer and a challenger. It is a reflection on how water's supple power can carve landscapes and sustain life, yet also unleash fury and reshape destinies.

A Mirror for Human Conduct: - Water serves as a mirror for our own conduct, urging us to evaluate our actions against its unmatched standard. It challenges us to rise to the occasion, to be *leaders* who can bring about change with the same grace and determination that water exhibits

The Alchemy of Harmony: - Just as hydrogen and oxygen, two volatile elements, come together to form water—a substance that extinguishes the very fires they might fuel—so too can rival nations find common ground. Through dialogue and consensus, they can overcome their differences and put out the fiery fire that burn their peace for prosperity that benefits all.

A Lesson in Diplomacy: - The poem serves as a lesson in diplomacy, illustrating how the merging of disparate forces can lead to outcomes that are greater than the sum of their parts. It is a call for nations and individuals alike to seek harmony over conflict, and to recognize the *strength that lies in diversity.*

Beauty Born from the Beastly: - The metaphor extends beyond the elemental, reflecting the potential for beauty to emerge from beastly origins. Flammable **Oxygen** and **Hydrogen** meet to form a substance that can put out the **flames of bane**. It is a testament to the power of transformation—the ability to turn rivalry into partnership, and conflict into collaboration.

"The Nonpareil Supple Power" is not merely a poem; it is a *blueprint for a more peaceful world.* It encourages us to look beyond our differences, to find the common humanity that binds us, and to work together towards a future where the *beauty of unity* outshines the fires of division. Let this poem inspire you to be an agent of change, fostering unity in diversity and creating a legacy of harmony for generations to come.

In the confluence of "The Nonpareil Supple Power" we find a harmonious symphony that speaks to the core of human existence and the transcendent power of unity.

20.   **What a Confused Feather Falling for the Floor!**

A bird in a cage had a lofty ambition,
To wing it, to fling it, to sing it, to swing it
To cloud nine, to sunshine, to moonshine, to starshine
To breeze and to freeze and to sneeze and to please

But the sky was a pie in the sky; a big lie!
It stormed and rained, and it pained and it stained
It hawked and it eagled and it owled and it vultured
And it sheltered no feather, no weather, no leather, no heather!

So the bird became a nerd, an engineer
To bridge gaps, to map laps, to tap taps, to rap raps
It'd better the world, and fetter the world,
and letter the world, still netter the world
To solve and to revolve and to evolve and to involve

But the engineer was a mere career, a veneer
It stressed and it pressed and it messed and it guessed
It ruled and it schooled and it fooled and it cooled
It freed no need, no deed, no seed, no mead

So the engineer became a healer, a doctor
To mend and to tend and to fend and to send
He'd healthify and wealthify the world,
he'd selfify the world, and stealthify the world
To aid and braid and to trade every jade

But the doctor was a proctor, a rocker, and a shocker
He bled and fed and led and even dead
He risked and he frisked and he whisked and he brisked
He peaced no lease, no grease, no fleece, no geese

So the doctor became a counter, an accountant
To sum every hum and to drum and to crumb
To enrich the world, to switch the world,
to stitch the world, to ditch the world
To smarten and to part and to dart and to art

But the accountant was a mount, a fount, a count
The bird numbered and it lumbered and it cumbered and it slumbered
It taxed and it axed and it maxed and it waxed
It meant no bent, no rent, no tent, no vent

So the accountant became a mentor, a teacher
To learn and to earn and to turn and to burn
To wise up the world, to size up the world,
to prize up the world, to rise up the world
To kindle and to spindle and to dwindle and to swindle

But the teacher was a preacher, a leecher, a bleacher
It taught and it fought and it bought and it wrought
It studented and it parented and it dented and it vented
It respected no sect, no project, no object, no subject

So the teacher became a mover, a bus driver
To steer and to veer and to cheer and to beer
To shrink the world, to link the world,
to wink the world, to sync the world
To calm and to palm and to balm and to psalm

But the bus driver was a diver, a survivor, a reviver
It storied and it gloried and it loried and it oried
It passengered and it friend and it family and it pet
It funned and it sunned and it gunned and it run

A Feather's Flight: Navigating Life's Absurdities

"What a Confused Feather Falling for the Floor" is a playful and insightful exploration of the human condition. Through a series of rapid-fire rhymes and witty observations, the poem delves into the complexities of identity, ambition, and the search for meaning.

The poem's central metaphor of the bird striving for flight but ultimately finding itself grounded is a relatable and humorous exploration of the gap between aspirations and reality. The bird's journey through a series of professions - engineer, doctor, accountant, teacher, and bus driver - mirrors the often circuitous path that individuals take in search of fulfillment, from the time they are young. They are not certain of what to follow, but inspired by everything. Resolve is however required, since one can never claim to be a professional swimmer, when they live in a desert with no swimming pool, for all their lives.

The poem's rapid-fire delivery creates a sense of breathlessness and chaos, reflecting the frenetic pace of modern life. The juxtaposition of lofty ambitions with mundane realities is a poignant commentary on the human condition.

The inclusion of humor in the poem is a strategic choice. By adopting a lighthearted tone, the poet is able to explore serious themes without overwhelming the reader. Laughter can serve as a powerful coping mechanism, allowing us to process difficult emotions in a healthier way.

"What a Confused Feather Falling for the Floor" is a reminder that life is full of unexpected twists and turns. It is a celebration of the human spirit's ability to adapt and find meaning in even the most ordinary of circumstances. The poem encourages us to embrace the absurdity of life and to find humor in our shared experiences.

While the poem might seem frivolous at first glance, it offers a deeper reflection on the human condition. The bird's journey through various professions can be seen as a metaphor for the search for identity and purpose. The ultimate realization that fulfillment can be found in the simplest of things - being a bus driver, connecting with people - is a profound message about the importance of human connection.

v.   The Silent Cry

The world is witnessing an alarming surge in youth suicides. This is a stark reflection of the silent crisis plaguing our generation. Beneath the surface of seemingly carefree youth, a cauldron of pressures, expectations, and societal constructs that are taking a devastating toll on mental health are a silent killer.

The Weight of Expectations: - Today's youth navigate a complex landscape fraught with challenges. Academic excellence, career aspirations, and societal norms converge to create an overwhelming pressure to succeed. The constant pursuit of perfection, often fueled by social media comparisons, can lead to feelings of inadequacy and worthlessness.

Furthermore, the traditional gender roles and expectations placed on young people have evolved, creating new strains. While the empowerment of women is a significant stride, it has inadvertently shifted the focus away from the boy child. Raised in an environment that often prioritizes female achievements, young men are left grappling with identity crises and a lack of emotional support. The expectation to embody maturity and leadership without adequate preparation exacerbates their vulnerability to mental health issues.

The Impact of Societal Pressures: - Beyond personal challenges, societal issues contribute to the mental health crisis among youth. Economic hardships, political instability, and social inequality can create a sense of uncertainty and hopelessness. The fear of failing to meet societal expectations, coupled with limited opportunities, can be overwhelming.

Moreover, the prevalence of cyberbullying and online harassment has created a toxic environment for young people. The constant exposure to negativity and hate speech can erode self-esteem and contribute to feelings of isolation.

Addressing the youth mental health crisis requires a multifaceted approach. It is imperative to create a supportive and understanding environment where young people feel comfortable expressing their emotions without fear of judgment. Schools, families, and communities must prioritize mental health education and awareness.

Furthermore, it is crucial to challenge traditional gender roles and expectations. Boys and young men should be encouraged to seek help and express their emotions openly. Mental health services should be accessible and affordable for all, regardless of socioeconomic status.

Ultimately, preventing youth suicides requires a collective effort. By fostering empathy, compassion, and understanding, we can create a society where young people feel supported and empowered to overcome their challenges. Let us break the silence surrounding mental health and work towards a future where every young person has the opportunity to thrive.

The alarming rates of youth suicide necessitate comprehensive and multifaceted solutions. The process should be deliberate enough, engaging enough, and supportive enough. Two school going children with come together and get pregnant; the young male will get a penance of some juvenile or even jail time while the female counterpart will get all the support, emotionally and financially to ensure save delivery. Her education will also be funded by well-wisher, while the dreams of the boy are cut short. I am not saying that she should not be supported.

My argument is, the boy child should be supported as well, educated about sexuality, and accountability, so that we achieve balance. Many divorces, flopped marriages and discord at home with depressed child stem not in the changing time but neglect for boy child.

Addressing Systemic Issues

Redefining Gender Roles: Promote gender equality without neglecting the needs of boys. Implement programs that foster emotional intelligence, resilience, and leadership skills in young men.

Comprehensive Sex Education: Equip young people with knowledge about sexuality, relationships, and consent. This can help prevent unintended pregnancies, sexually transmitted infections, and emotional distress.

Economic Empowerment: Create job opportunities and entrepreneurship programs for youth to alleviate financial pressures and provide a sense of purpose.

Social Safety Nets: Implement policies that address poverty, inequality, and social injustice, which are often underlying factors contributing to mental health issues.

Increased Accessibility: Expand mental health services, making them affordable and accessible to all young people, regardless of socioeconomic status.

Early Intervention: Implement mental health screening programs in schools and communities to identify and address issues early on.

Stigma Reduction: Challenge the stigma surrounding mental health through education and awareness campaigns.

Holistic Approach: Promote physical health, nutrition, and sleep as essential components of mental well-being.

Life Skills Education: Teach young people coping mechanisms, stress management techniques, and problem-solving skills.

Mentorship Programs: Connect youth with positive role models who can provide guidance and support.

Social and Emotional Learning: Incorporate social and emotional learning into school curricula to develop empathy, communication, and relationship-building skills.

Digital Literacy: Educate young people about the potential negative impacts of social media and teach them how to use technology responsibly.

Parental Involvement: Empower parents with knowledge and resources to support their children's mental health.

Community Engagement: Foster collaboration between schools, healthcare providers, community organizations, and youth to create a supportive network.

Peer Support: Encourage peer support groups where young people can share experiences and provide mutual support.

The Final Destination is more than a collection of poems; it is a call to action, an invitation to explore the depths of the human experience and to find meaning and purpose in our lives. Through vivid imagery and raw emotion, I offer you a profound reflection on the complexities of the human condition, from the exhilaration of hope to the depths of despair.

Resilience: The Cornerstone of the Human Spirit

One of the central themes that emerges from this collection is resilience. The ability to withstand, overcome, and learn from adversity is a hallmark of the human spirit. As the psychologist Viktor Frankl observed in his book *"Man's Search for Meaning,"* even in the most extreme circumstances, humans possess an inner strength that allows them to find purpose and hope.

The world we live in recognizes strength. The weak are preyed upon. But how do you develop this strength/ look beyond your current dismay. Walk through that fog of reality. Sweep through the neglect, through the stigma, through the woes, and erect your flag high enough to claim your spot. I am not saying that you will not falter. To win the race will depend on how quick you will spring up after a fall. Even Lions and bears crave a little love and a hug. But one thing I know is that lions do not eat grass. They'd rather die. Never compromise your integrity for affinity. This is your DNA, and the currency you will trade for victory

I invite you, the readers, to cultivate resilience by embracing challenges as opportunities for growth. Just as the metaphorical "bird" in *"What a Confused Feather Falling for the Floor"* adapts to its circumstances, we too can find strength and purpose in the face of adversity. One of the greatest lesson I learn from flowing water is its ability to adapt, physically, chemically and biologically. As the greatest architect, water curves stones and meanders of the greatest river, not because of its brute force but through perseverance, resilience and adaptation. That is why we have water everywhere. And water can be made from almost anything. Be fluid, be adaptable, be resilient, and you will navigate the intricacies of this cruel world. Most important to remember from all this, leave a mark, just like water does, without the brute force of a diamond or a chisel which is depended on human hands.

The Power of Human Connection

Another overarching theme in the collection is the importance of human connection. The poems emphasize the need for empathy, understanding, and compassion in our relationships with others. As the philosopher Martin Buber noted, *"I can only exist as a person in relation to other people."* Our interactions with others shape our identity and contribute to our overall well-being.

The poems also highlight the significance of support networks in navigating life's challenges. By sharing our experiences and vulnerabilities, we create a sense of community and belonging. As the psychoanalyst Carl Jung observed, "The meeting of two personalities is like the contact of two chemical substances: if there is any reaction, both are transformed."

Remember that, in this world, where you can be anything, where you can do anything, it would cost you nothing to be nice. You never know what that kind word you utter, or that encouragement you give, can do. The souls of men are like an island; a solitary continent with its own climate, its own seasons, and its own topography. Only the native inhabitant truly knows its contours.

The Search for Meaning and Purpose

I implore you to start contemplating the meaning of life and the search for purpose in a new way of cyclical fluidity. We have explored the complexities of human existence, from the exhilaration of achievement to the despair of loss. As the existential philosopher Albert Camus wrote, *"The only serious philosophical question is suicide. Judging whether life is or is not worth living amounts to answering the fundamental question of philosophy."*

As you wonder what your space is, in this callous unforgiving world, remember that what you are is a culmination of myriad decisions. Every single decision, not matter how small it might seem: choosing to brush your teeth, choosing to extend some greetings to a stranger, choosing to start a business, choosing to run for presidency; all these infinitesimal and giant decisions you make are your true self. Be intentional to succeed. It starts in the morning, by choosing not to ignore the alarm clock, and by choosing to take a heavy breakfast for the day, and choosing not to smoke that weed that is so enticing with ethereal serenity. Choose to live, choose to win, chose to succeed.

Embracing the Journey

Ultimately, "Final Destination" is a celebration of the human journey, with all its joys, sorrows, and complexities. The poems invite readers to embrace the ups and downs of life with courage and resilience. As the poet Rainer Maria Rilke wrote, *"The only journey is the one within."* Turns and twists are inevitable. Failures are a sure bet, but at that instant you can choose to go back to the start and purchase brand new tickets, or alter the course of your journey.

Remember that every journey will have a destination and you are the author of it all. Choosing a slightly different path, subtly a shorter one, sadly a longer one, will not hinder you from your destination. All I ask is that you do not chose the destination of the speaker in *'Final destination'*. There is much we can do before the eventful day.

By exploring the themes of resilience, human connection, and the search for meaning, this collection offers readers a roadmap for navigating life's challenges. It is a reminder that we are not alone in our struggles and that there is hope to be found in even the darkest of times.

This collection of poems is a poignant and multifaceted exploration of the human condition, navigating the complexities of life with raw honesty and lyrical depth. From the depths of despair to the heights of hope, these verses offer a profound reflection on the human experience, inviting readers to embark on a journey of self-discovery and empathy.

The poems serve as a powerful reminder that we are all connected by shared experiences, and that in our shared humanity, we can find solace, strength, and inspiration.

Like the phoenix rising from the ashes, the collection demonstrates the capacity of the human spirit to endure and transcend adversity. The poems, much like the works of poets such as Maya Angelou, who found solace and strength in the face of adversity, offer a beacon of hope in the darkest of times.

This exploration of mental health in poems like "Beyond the Shadows" is particularly commendable. By giving voice to the often unspoken struggles of the human mind, it contributes to a broader conversation about mental well-being and destigmatize. This work echoes the sentiments of writers like Virginia Woolf, who delved into the complexities of the human psyche with unflinching honesty.

"What a Confused Feather Falling for the Floor" adds a layer of complexity and depth to the collection. It demonstrates one's ability to find light even in the darkest of times, a quality akin to the resilience showcased in other poems. The poem, much like the works of poets such as Shel Silverstein, who used humor to explore profound themes, offers a unique perspective on the human experience.

This collection invites readers to reflect on their own lives and experiences. It encourages empathy, understanding, and a deeper appreciation for the complexities of the human condition. By sharing This vulnerabilities and triumphs, you can create a space for connection and shared experience.

As you close the final page of "The Final Destination and Other Poems," you embark on a journey that extends far beyond the confines of these words. This collection has invited you to explore the depths of the human soul, to confront the complexities of life, and to find meaning in the midst of chaos.

The poems within these pages have served as a mirror, reflecting the triumphs and tribulations of the human experience. They have offered solace, inspiration, and a sense of connection with others who share your journey.

But this journey does not end here. As you close the book, you are invited to carry its lessons forward, to integrate them into your own life. Let the themes of resilience, hope, and human connection guide you on your path.

Remember, life is a constant journey, filled with twists and turns, triumphs and setbacks. Like the characters in these poems, you too might face challenges, experience loss, and discover moments of pure joy. But it is in the navigating of this journey that we find meaning and purpose.

As you embark on the next chapter of your own story, let these poems serve as a compass, guiding you towards a life of fulfillment and authenticity. Embrace the complexities of the human experience, cultivate resilience, and seek connection with others.

The journey may be long and arduous, but the destination is worth the effort. For in the end, it is not about reaching a specific goal but about the growth and transformation that occurs along the way.